KINGDOM EVANGELISM

FRESH FIRE

BY
DR. BOBBY G. MCALLISTER

ISBN:1-59352-074-3

Published by:
Christian Services Network
1975 Janich Ranch Ct.
El Cajon, CA 92019
Toll Free: 1-866-484-6184

Printed in the United States of America

WHAT OTHERS ARE SAYING

About Kingdom Evangelism: Fresh Fire

It's a joy and honor to present and recommend one of the best books I have ever read, *Kingdom Evangelism: Fresh Fire.* You will not be able to put this book down. This book will show you how to overcome the enemy's tactics and fulfill God's plan for your life.

Dr. J. L. Cook, Ph.D., President
North Carolina College of Theology

Kingdom Evangelism Fresh Fire, is both unique and inspiring because the "Message" has become the "Messenger." The messenger has been sent to the nations by God to bring his gift of wholeness to the body of Christ. The Word has been applied on the tablet of Dr. McAllister's heart, and is now the written epistle, the Word in the flesh, an open book read by all. [The complete Foreword by Dr. Veverly Wyche starts on page 11 of this book.]

Dr. Veverly Wyche
IMAGO DEI MINISTRIES
Freehold, NJ

iii

DEDICATION

This book is dedicated to my wife Dorothy, my daughter Laquesha, Jacqueline Walker, my Administrative Secretary, and Timothy Walker, my cover designer. Also, to the Elders, Deacons, and Congregation of the Justice Fellowship International Inc, Worship & Training Center, and the Apostles for their prayers, patience, and faithful support.

It is also dedicated to the Justice Fellowship International Network and Justice Fellowship College of Theology, Jacksonville, North Carolina.

FOREWORD

Kingdom Evangelism Fresh Fire, is both unique and inspiring because the "Message" has become the "Messenger." The messenger has been sent to the nations by God to bring his gift of wholeness to the body of Christ. The Word has been applied on the tablet of Dr. McAllister's heart, and is now the written epistle, the Word in the flesh, an open book read by all.

Dr. McAllister writes about the anointed Evangelist whose lifestyle consumes and purifies men's consciousness. The Kingdom Evangelist deposits life that brings an awakening to the new identity, "Christ in you the hope of glory." This new man reproduces as he spreads the good news, (the message of the Kingdom); righteousness, peace and joy in the Holy Ghost. As the message is spread, healing to the nations is given, and the life of Christ overflows out of the temple.

Man's old nature has been consumed, and you now have a new creation walking in the earth. This new creation manifests God's nature of holiness and righteousness (one set apart to bring all unto God). There is an "INEXPRESSIBLE JOY" that radiates from this Evangelistic vessel. It is God's "MINISTERING ANGEL OF FIRE" that will draw all of humanity with God's everlasting Love. This Ministering Angel of fire is Gods Evangelists for such a time as this, the 21st Century. There has never been a day like this before, where the "anointed one" is appearing in our midst, destroying yokes and setting the captives free.

The great commission has now become the greatest commandment: "To love thy neighbor as thyself." Fresh fire depicts a manifestation of God in the earth that cuts across every racial, religious, and economic boundary. There are no walls or limitations with this Evangelist.

The world is hungry for the Kingdom Evangelist. The world has been waiting for the manifestation of the sons of God to come forth. The world is ready to receive the Son; "Manifested in the Body of Christ as one new man, known as Love."

And we have known and believed the love that God hath to us. God is love; and he that dwelleth in love dwelleth in God, and God in him.

(I John 4:16, KJV)

Dr. Veverly Wyche
IMAGO DEI MINISTRIES
Freehold, NJ

INTRODUCTION

The Church and the world are quickly moving into the "Third Day of God." Everything is rapidly changing! We witness these changes taking place in everything and everywhere in the home, the marketplace, the rich, the poor, the young, and the old. During this change, many people are wandering, aimlessly without purpose, because they don't feel like they are a part of what's happening: the change. Those who are wandering aimlessly fail to realize that the earth is the Lord's, and it all belongs to Him, including the world and the people that dwell in it.

Because He has called us to be lords and kings in His earth that we live in, Evangelism must take place to ensure that we fulfill our call of being "lords and kings in the earth." This evangelism is not necessarily the Evangelism of the past, but it is the evangelism of the Kingdom. Jesus defined the Evangelistic plan of the Kingdom when he answered the question, "Which is the great commandment in the Law?"

*Thou shalt love the Lord thy God with all they heart, and with all thy soul, and with all thy mind. This is the first and great commandment. And the second is like unto it, Thou shalt **love thy neighbor as thyself**. On these two commandments hang all the law and the prophets.*

(Matt. 22:35-40)

Jesus' plan of Evangelism is much more simplistic than we currently understand. **<u>Kingdom Evangelism is a lifestyle that's developed and manifested through relationships</u>**. Jesus clearly outlines those relationships in his answer, "Love the Lord and love yourself so that you can love your neighbor." The Evangelism necessary for today emanates out of a lifestyle of love. This is the Evangelism that must be administered this day for all mankind to fulfill the call of God on their lives of being lords and kings in the earth today.

> *This is the Day of the Lord and to be truly effective in this hour, the Law of Love must be actively at work in God's people.*
> (Matt. 22:37-40)

The Love of the Lord is revealed in "threes," and is based on relationships:

The first and most crucial relationship is with the Lord. Without first establishing a relationship with God, it is impossible to fulfill the second half of the great commandment of loving your neighbor as yourself, because God is love.

Therefore, in order to love, you must first experience, possess, and be in relationship with Love. *Anything else is lust at best, need-oriented and motivated by selfishness.*

Loving the Lord requires knowing that He loves you, lives in your heart, and He has satisfied the desires of your soul *(intellect, will, and emotions)*. He has given you the mind of Christ, whereby you may live and function in the earth daily.

The revealing of God must be understood to know who He is and how He has accomplished all of these miracles within you.

For God so loved the world, that he gave his only begotten Son, that whosoever believeth in him should not perish, but have everlasting life.

For God sent not his Son into the world to condemn the world; but that the world through him might be saved.
(John 3:16-17 KJV)

Dr. Bobby G. McAllister

x

TABLE OF CONTENTS

CHAPTER ONE

New Wine
"Christ is the Anointing"

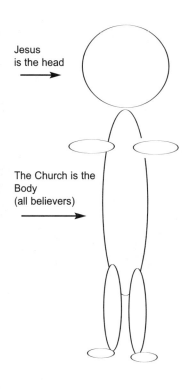

Jesus
is the head

The Church is the
Body
(all believers)

There is a new man standing. This new man has traveled the road of transition to transformation. The old man has been revealed and removed, and now we are in final pursuit. The foundation has been laid. We have founded our place and are aware that the new wine is found in the cluster. The glory of God has come down in us, upon us, and among us making us one according to the prayerful desire of Jesus in John 17. Together we shall enter into the City of the Living God.

New Wine is found! In this changing world, our hearts must be open to experience something new. In this new experience we will be changed into the same image of God, from glory to glory, even as by the spirit of the Lord. For where the spirit of the Lord is, there is liberty and a progressive understanding.

This new wine will not fit into the old wineskins; there must be a new order. Remember, God is not the author of confusion. This new order is of peace and not of war. (Mark 2:21-22)

> *Thus saith the LORD, as the new wine is found in the cluster, and one saith, Destroy it not; for a blessing is in it: so will I do for my servants' sakes, that I may not destroy them all.*
>
> (Isa. 65:8)

The Glory of God can only be found in the body of Christ. Therefore, we must learn to function together to experience His glory.

The pattern must be sealed with the Glory of God and the glory shall be revealed in the temple that is built according to the pattern.

- The Lord Jesus Christ is both, God's Tabernacle and God's Temple. He was perfect in all He was, all He thought, all He said, and all He did. He measured up perfectly to God's pattern for man.

- The seal of God was upon Him and the glory indwelt Him in fullness. On the Mount of Transfiguration the Glory of God shone through the Veil of His Flesh. In John chapter 17, He asks the Father to clothe Him with the Glory He had before the world began.

4

The city of God is sealed by the glory of the light of God and his Christ. It is a city whose builder and maker is God.
                                (Hebrews 11:10-16)

This New Testament Church will be according to the divine pattern and the end result will be that the Glory of God will fill the EARTH. This is the divine seal on the finished work that is built according to the pattern.

Thou shalt arise, and have mercy upon Zion: for the time to favour her, yea, the set time, is come. For thy servants take pleasure in her stones, and favour the dust thereof. So the heathen shall fear the name of the LORD, and all the kings of the earth thy glory. When the LORD shall build up Zion, he shall appear in his glory.
                                (Ps. 102:13-16)

In this New Day, we must:

- Have a sure foundation

- Be established in present truth and understand body positioning

- Be a team with an "energy to finish mentality"

- See the vision (the person) not the project

Where there is no revelation, the people cast off restraint; but blessed is he who keeps the law.
                                (Prov. 29:18 NIV)

YOU CAN HAVE THE PATTERN AND NOT THE GLORY, BUT YOU CANNOT HAVE THE GLORY WITHOUT THE PATTERN.

CHAPTER TWO

GoLocal Vision Requirement

For though ye have ten thousand instructors in Christ, yet have ye not many fathers: for in Christ Jesus I have begotten you through the gospel.

(1 Cor. 4:15)

Evangelism in the third day is the experience of living out of the Lord daily with His mind for the purpose of re-gathering the sons unto their fathers. Once sons are gathered unto fathers, they are placed into position and are used as a corporate expression to positively effect change in the Global Economy.

You must know who your father is according to God's choosing. There is a Fathering Order that is needed for Godly transition. There are three things both natural and spiritual that you cannot choose:

- The Father that God gave you

- The Mother that God gave you (Local Church Leadership)

- The Family you where born into (Local Church Body)

THE ILLUSTRATION OF THE FATHERING ORDER:

Natural Father:	Flesh and Blood
Nurturing Father:	Practical Teacher in the Natural
Teachers:	Instructors in Natural Things

= = = = = = = = = = = = = = = = = = === = = = = = = = =

Spiritual Father:	Passover, by the Word
Nurturing Father:	Passover, Practical Teacher
Teachers:	Instructors in The Faith and Righteousness

= =

Spiritual Father: Pentecost, by the
                          Spirit

Nurturing Father: Pentecost,
                          Practical
                          Teacher

Teachers: Instructors in
                          The Holy Spirit

= =

Spiritual Father: Tabernacles, by
                          Impartation

Nurturing Father: Tabernacles,
                          Practical Teacher

Teachers: Instructors in
                          The Life of God

= =

CHAPTER THREE

Life of God From Within

God is revealed in Passover; the born again experience, Pentecost; experiencing the baptism of the Holy Spirit, and Tabernacles; the mind of Christ experiencing the liberty of living out the life of Christ daily. Therefore, there must be a crossing over in our thinking. We must begin to experience Him from within and not just see Him in the external. He must be personified, made known, and visible.

A psalmist sings:

"You were born to be His dwelling place
A home for the presence of the Lord
So let your life now be separated unto Thee
That you might be what you were born to be."

WE MUST CROSS OVER AND MAKE A DECISION TO ENTER THE DAY OF THE LORD.

There are multitudes (God's People) in the Valley of Decision. They must come to a determination about God, who He is and how He makes Himself known. God is making demands on our lives. We must decide which way to go, with Him or without Him. There is NO middle ground. God is working salvation in the midst of the earth in and through his people.

11

Multitudes, multitudes in the valley of decision: for the day of the LORD is near in the valley of decision.

(Joel 3:14 KJV)

We have this treasure in earthen vessels, that the excellency of the power may be of God, and not of us...

(2 Cor. 4:7 KJV)

For our conversation is in heaven; from whence also we look for the Saviour, the Lord Jesus Christ.

(Phil. 3:20 KJV)

The LORD shall reign for ever, even thy God, O Zion, unto all generations. Praise ye the LORD.

(Ps. 146:10 KJV)

ALL TRUTH IS FOUND IN THREE DIMENSIONS (DEPTHS OF THREES).

Three times in a year *shall all thy males appear before the LORD thy God* ***in the place which he shall choose;*** *in* ***the feast of unleavened bread,*** *and in the feast of weeks, and in the* ***feast of tabernacles:*** *and they shall not appear before the LORD empty. Every man shall give as he is able, according to the blessing of the LORD thy God which he hath given thee.*

(Deut. 16:16-17)

But we had the sentence of death in ourselves, that we should not trust in ourselves, but in God which raiseth the dead: Who delivered us from so great a death, and doth deliver: in whom we trust that he will yet deliver us.

(2 Cor. 1:9-10)

Jesus saith unto him, **I am the way, the truth, and the life:** *no man cometh unto the Father, but by me.*

(John 14:6)

He made known his ways unto Moses, his acts unto the children of Israel.

(Ps. 103:7 KJV)

WE MUST SEEK TO KNOW HIS WAYS, AND AS WE DO, WE MUST LOVE OUR NEIGHBORS AS OURSELVES.

The greater question is: **"Who is my Neighbor?"**

A <u>NEIGHBOR</u> is a friend, close associate, or a person who lives nearby. The Abrahamic Covenant established moral obligations among the Israelites. They were commanded to show concern for their neighbors (Gen. 12:1-3). The ninth and tenth commandments prohibited the defaming or slandering of a neighbor and condemned the envying of a neighbor's wife, servant, livestock, or other possessions. **(Ex. 20:16-17; Deut. 5:20-21)**

For this, Thou shalt not commit adultery, Thou shalt not kill, Thou shalt not steal, Thou shalt not bear false witness, Thou shalt not covet; and if there be any other commandment, it is briefly comprehended in this saying, namely, Thou shalt love thy neighbour as thyself. Love worketh no ill to his neighbour: therefore love is the fulfilling of the law.

(Rom. 13:9-10 KJV)

We must understand that the fulfillment of the New Testament cannot be made manifest by man. It's manifested only by the Power of God, not by the written scripture, but by the Resurrection Power of God from within, *Christ in you.* It takes the Power of God for you to fulfill the second great commandment.

Thou shalt love thy neighbour as thyself. On these two commandments hang all the law and the prophets.

(Matt. 22:35-40 KJV)

Jesus extended the concept of neighbor to include strangers, as in the parable of the Good Samaritan and hence all mankind. (Luke 10:25-37)

The apostle Paul declared that loving your neighbor as yourself was a supreme commandment. (Rom. 13:9-10, Luke 10:25-37)

Loving your neighbor is an extension of the rule of God in the earth through a people, *the House of God, The Church.*

The second relationship implied within the second great commandment is to love yourself. Loving yourself requires the total giving of yourself. As an Evangelist functioning out of the Kingdom, you must be a GIVER. Giving and loving go hand in hand. God demonstrated this principle when he prepared the way of redemption for us before the foundation of the world through his Son Jesus. Because He is Love, He gave.

*For God so **loved** the world, that he **gave** his only begotten **Son,** that whosoever believeth in him should not perish, but have*

everlasting life. For God sent not his Son into the world to condemn the world; but that the world through him might be saved.
(John 3:16-17 KJV)

This scripture reveals God's heart towards mankind, and that the attitude, nature and character of God is love. Love is always giving. Love seeks for places and opportunities to give, seeking to fulfill our call to be lords and kings in the earth. We too must be givers, and out of love, seek for places and opportunities to give.

God is never a taker. His heart has always been to give. Understanding what it truly means to be lords and kings, allows us to know that we are part owners of all things in God. Knowing this will prevent us from **attempting** to rob God. He is an Honorable Father. (Mal. 3:8-9)

- Bring the tithes into the storehouse
- Be filled with the Holy Ghost
- Have the mind of Christ

Jesus fulfilled the law and removed the curse. However, it's through our obedience that we appropriate all that He has. You cannot be disobedient in the area of giving, because the place of agreement is the place of power. We must agree with God and His will. Our agreement with God and our love toward Him is demonstrated through the keeping of His commandments to love.

YOU MUST HONOR THE LORD

Honour the LORD with thy substance, and with the firstfruits of all thine increase: So

15

*shall thy barns be filled with plenty, and thy
presses shall burst out with new wine.*
(Prov. 3:9-10 KJV)

You must honor the Lord by honoring the man or
woman of God that begot you and shepherded you.
There must be a place and a person for you to bring
and present yourself as a tithe and an offering before
you present your money.

*And be not drunk with wine, wherein is excess;
but be filled with the Spirit; Speaking to
yourselves in psalms and hymns and spiritual
songs, singing and making melody in your
heart to the Lord; Giving thanks always for all
things unto God and the Father in the name of
our Lord Jesus Christ; Submitting yourselves
one to another in the fear of God.*
(Eph. 5:18-21 KJV)

The trial of giving exposes our true colors. People
that are true givers are incredibly happy even if they
are desperately poor.

**THE TRUE EVANGELISTIC SPIRIT IS THE
SPIRIT OF ONENESS. THEY ONLY SEE ONE,
THE BODY**.

*This is a great mystery: but I speak concerning
Christ and the church.*
(Eph. 5:32 KJV)

SEVEN PRINCIPLES TO GIVING HONOR

1. You must be a giver.

2. You must love people beyond what you see.

16

3. You must see them whole, without condemnation.

4. Love them even if they appear to be your enemy.

5. Give of yourself when it's undeserved.

6. Be filled with the Spirit with a manifestation of the Righteousness, Peace, and Joy in the Holy Ghost.

7. Announce to them that they are already saved if they believe.

The Kingdom Evangelist doesn't look for formulas, but speaks the truth declaring to humanity they were saved in Him before the foundation of the world. All they need to do is believe. When they believe, the Transitional Reality (going from one degree of understanding in God to another) begins.

When an unbeliever is led to Christ, the local church must follow through with engrafting the new convert into the body. New converts must feel that the local church is a safe and loving environment.

A TRUE SENSE OF A PROTECTIVE COVERING IS A POWERFUL EVANGELISTIC TOOL.

We must understand that babies cannot be left alone without nurturing. They must be engrafted into a local church and the body of Christ for nurturing and growth.

Luke 6:27-28 states that you must,

...love your enemies, do good to them which

hate you. Bless them that curse you, and pray for them which despitefully use you.

Be ye therefore merciful, as your Father also is merciful. Judge not, and ye shall not be judged: condemn not, and ye shall not be condemned: forgive, and ye shall be forgiven: Give, and it shall be given unto you; good measure, pressed down, and shaken together, and running over, shall men give into your bosom. For with the same measure that ye mete withal it shall be measured to you again.

(Luke 6:36-38 KJV)

GOD'S DESIRE IS FOR US TO BE WHOLE IN OUR UNDERSTANDING: SPIRIT, SOUL, AND BODY.

CHAPTER FOUR

Kingdom Pronouncement

WE MUST DECLARE:

I'm the life of God in the earth, for the whole world to see. I'm the son of my Father, **God**, with His life as my credentials. I'm part owner of everything that is real because we are heirs of God and joint heirs with Jesus. **This is who I am! An heir and a son of God**.

> *For the promise, that he should be the heir of the world, was not to Abraham, or to his seed, through the law, but through the righteousness of faith.*
>
> (Rom. 4:13)

> *[God] Hath in these last days spoken unto us by his Son, whom he hath appointed heir of all things, by whom also he made the worlds.*
>
> (Heb. 1:2 KJV)

WE MUST WALK BY FAITH

> *By faith Noah, being warned of God of things not seen as yet, moved with fear, prepared an ark to the saving of his house; by which he condemned the world, and became heir of the righteousness, which is by faith.*
>
> (Heb. 11:7 KJV)

WE HAVE BEEN CALLED–JUSTIFIED–GLORIFIED

For whom he did foreknow, he also did predestinate to be conformed to the image of his Son, that he might be the firstborn among many brethren. Moreover whom he did predestinate, them he also called: and whom he called, them he also justified: and whom he justified, them he also glorified.
(Rom. 8:29-30 KJV)

The Truth is **NOW, when I have believed it,** although it has been truth before the foundation of the world.

That in the dispensation of the fullness of times he might gather together in one all things in Christ, both which are in heaven, and which are on earth; even in him:
(Eph. 1:10 KJV)

For this is the covenant that I will make with the house of Israel after those days, saith the Lord; I will put my laws into their mind, and write them in their hearts: and I will be to them a God, and they shall be to me a people: And they shall not teach every man his neighbour, and every man his brother, saying, Know the Lord: for all shall know me, from the least to the greatest.
(Heb. 8:10-11 KJV)

Then said he, Lo, I come to do thy will, O God. He taketh away the first, that he may establish the second.
(Heb. 10:9 KJV)

Not forsaking the assembling of ourselves together, as the manner of some is; but exhorting one another: and so much the more, as ye see the day approaching.

(Heb. 10:25 KJV)

THIS IS A CALL TO RAISE THE STANDARD

"Go through the gates." Go through, go through the gates; prepare ye the way of the people; cast up, cast up the highway; gather out the stones; lift up a standard for the people.*

(Isaiah 62:10 KJV)

1. Go through the Gates.
2. Prepare ye the way of the people.
3. Cast up the highway, the Way of Holiness.
4. Gather out the stones.
5. Lift up a standard for the people.

Behold, the LORD hath proclaimed unto the end of the world, Say ye to the daughter of Zion, Behold, thy salvation cometh; behold, his reward is with him, and his work before him. And they shall call them, <u>The holy people</u>, <u>The redeemed</u> of the LORD: and thou shalt be called, <u>Sought out</u>, <u>A city not Forsaken</u>.

(Isaiah 62:11-12 KJV)

CHAPTER FIVE

Kingdom Evangelist

WHO IS HE?
- A many-membered man.

WHAT SHALL HE DO?
- Declare "the Kingdom of God is here."

HOW SHALL HE DO IT?
- By the words of life.

The Kingdom Evangelist must flow with an Apostolic Anointing *(one sent)*. The Kingdom Evangelist must declare the finished work of Jesus; "It's a done deal."

HE MUST BE ABLE TO MINISTER IN ALL THREE DIMENSIONS: PASSOVER, PENTECOST, TABERNACLE.

When Jesus therefore had received the vinegar, he said, It is finished: and he bowed his head, and gave up the ghost.
(John 19:30 KJV)

GOD ALWAYS REVEALS HIMSELF THROUGH MAN; A PERSON IN HIS IMAGE.

So God created man in his own image, in the image of God created He him; male and female created he them.
(Gen. 1:27 KJV)

GOD HAS ALWAYS HAD A PLAN AND PURPOSE. THE PURPOSE IS FOR MAN TO HAVE DOMINION OVER ALL CREATION.

And God blessed them, and God said unto them, Be fruitful, and multiply, and replenish the earth, and subdue it: and have dominion over the fish of the sea, and over the fowl of the air, and over every living thing that moveth upon the earth.
(Gen. 1:28 KJV)

GOD ALWAYS HAS A STRATEGY. THE MEANS IS BY REPRODUCTION.

THIS MAN MUST HAVE UNDERSTANDING OF THE "COMPLETE MAN."

And ye are complete in him, which is the head of all principality and power.
(Colossians 2:10 KJV)

THIS MAN IS A MANY-MEMBERED MAN CREATED IN THE IMAGE OF GOD.

THIS MAN MUST BE A SON WITH THE LIKENESS, NATURE, AND CHARACTER OF GOD.

HE MUST SOUND LIKE GOD OR CREATION WILL NOT RECOGNIZE HIM.

THIS MAN MUST SPEAK WITH THE AUTHORITY OF GOD, AS ONE SENT FROM GOD.

THIS MAN MUST DECLARE THE KINGDOM OF GOD NOT ONLY IN WORDS,

BUT ALSO IN POWER THAT CHANGES LIVES BY HIS WORDS AND THE ANOINTING.

Then he answered and spake unto me, saying, This is the word of the LORD unto Zerubbabel, saying, Not by might, nor by power, but by my spirit, saith the LORD of hosts.

(Zech. 4:6 KJV)

THIS MAN MUST WALK IN FULL AGREEMENT WITH GOD, WALKING IN THE DOMINION IN WHICH GOD HAS GIVEN HIM IN THE EARTH.

Can two walk together, except they be agreed?
(Amos 3:3)

The earth is the LORD's, and the fulness thereof; the world, and they that dwell therein.

(Psalm 24:1 KJV)

THE EARTH IS THE LORD'S AND THE FULNESS THEREOF.

CHAPTER SIX

Fresh Fire: A Non-Stop Flame

Fire was used to consume the burnt offerings and the incense offering, beginning with the sacrifice of Noah (Gen. 8:20) and continuing in the ever-burning fire on the altar. In the sacrificial flame the essence of the animal was resolved into vapor; so that when a man presented a sacrifice in his own stead, his inmost being, his spirit, and his heart ascended to God in the vapor, and the sacrifice brought the feeling of his heart before God.

> *The altar of fire was miraculously sent from God, like the fire of Jehovah that consumed the sacrifices of David and Solomon.*
> (1 Chron. 21:26, 2 Chron. 7:1)

> *And Aaron lifted up his hand toward the people, and blessed them, and came down from offering the sin offering, and the burnt offering, and peace offerings. And Moses and Aaron went into the tabernacle of the congregation, and came out, and blessed the people: and the glory of the LORD appeared unto all the people. And there came a fire out from before the LORD, and consumed upon the altar the burnt offering and the fat: which when all the people saw, they shouted, and fell on their faces.*
> (Lev. 9:22-24 KJV)

The miracle recorded in this verse did not consist in the fact that the sacrificial offerings placed upon the altar were burned by fire which proceeded from Jehovah, but the sacrifices, which were already on fire, were suddenly consumed by it. Fire was to be constantly burning upon the altar without going out, so that the burnt offering might never go out, because this was the divinely appointed symbol and visible sign of the uninterrupted worship of Jehovah, which the covenant nation could never suspend, either day or night, without being unfaithful to its calling.

Jehovah appeared in the burning bush and on Mt. Sinai.

(Ex. 3:2; 19:18)

Fire is illustrative of:

- The church's overcoming her enemies (Ob. 18)
- The Word of God (Jer. 5:14; 23:29)
- The Holy Spirit (Isa. 4:4, Acts 2:2-4)

NON-STOP FLAME

And of the angels he saith, who maketh his angels spirits, and his ministers a flame of fire.

(Heb. 1:7 KJV)

CREATE IN ME A CLEAN HEART

Create in me a clean heart, O God; and renew a right spirit within me.

(Ps. 51:10 KJV)

INCREASE AND DECREASE

He must increase, but I must decrease.
(John 3:30 KJV)

THIS NEW COVENANT

But this shall be the covenant that I will make with the house of Israel; After those days, saith the LORD, I will put my law in their inward parts, and write it in their hearts; and I will be their God, and they shall be my people.
(Jer. 31:33 KJV)

WATER–SPIRIT–FIRE

I indeed baptize you with water unto repentance: but he that cometh after me is mightier than I, whose shoes I am not worthy to bear: he shall baptize you with the Holy Ghost, and with fire: Whose fan is in his hand, and he will thoroughly purge his floor, and gather his wheat into the garner; but he will burn up the chaff with unquenchable fire.
(Matt. 3:11-12 KJV)

We are the:

- Flame of God
- Fire of God
- Torch of God to the world to give them light

Let your light so shine before men, that they may see your good works, and glorify your Father which is in heaven.

I love them that love me; and those that seek me early shall find me. Riches and honour are with me; yea, durable riches and righteousness. My fruit is better than gold, yea, than fine gold; and my revenue than choice silver. I lead in the way of righteousness, in the midst of the paths of judgment: That I may cause those that love me to inherit substance; and I will fill their treasures.

(Prov. 8:17-21 KJV)

There must be a:

- Blessing
- Breaking
- Giving

For your shame ye shall have double; and for confusion they shall rejoice in their portion: therefore in their land they shall possess the double: everlasting joy shall be unto them.

(Isa. 61:7 KJV)

WE MUST UNDERSTAND THE WORD, THE WILL AND THE WAY OF THE LORD.

- THE WORD: The word was made flesh

And the Word was made flesh, and dwelt among us, (and we beheld his glory, the glory as of the only begotten of the Father,) full of grace and truth.

(John 1:14 KJV)

- THE WILL: God desires a family of sons like the first born

For whom he did foreknow, he also did predestinate to be conformed to the image of his Son, that he might be the firstborn among many brethren.

(Rom. 8:29 KJV)

- The Way: Reproduction by the spirit of the Living God

And Simon Peter answered and said, Thou art the Christ, the Son of the living God.
(Matt. 16:16 KJV)

Behold, I will send my messenger, and he shall prepare the way before me: and the Lord, whom ye seek, shall suddenly come to his temple, even the messenger of the covenant, whom ye delight in: behold, he shall come, saith the LORD of hosts. But who may abide the day of his coming? and who shall stand when he appeareth? for he is like a refiner's fire, and like fullers' soap: And he shall sit as a refiner and purifier of silver: and he shall purify the sons of Levi, and purge them as gold and silver, that they may offer unto the LORD an offering in righteousness.

(Mal. 3:1-3 KJV)

For our God is a consuming fire.
(Heb. 12:29)

The Holy Ghost

In the last day, that great day of the feast, Jesus stood and cried, saying, If any man thirst, let him come unto me, and drink. He that believeth on me, as the scripture hath said, out of his belly shall flow rivers of living water.

(John 7:37-38 KJV)

WE MUST HAVE HIS MIND, SO LET IT BE

Let this mind be in you, which was also in Christ Jesus: Who, being in the form of God, thought it not robbery to be equal with God:

(Phil. 2:5-6 KJV)

RIGHTEOUS MUST PREVAIL

But the day of the Lord will come as a thief in the night; in which the heavens shall pass away with a great noise, and the elements shall melt with fervent heat, the earth also and the works that are therein shall be burned up. Seeing then that all these things shall be dissolved, what manner of persons ought ye to be in all holy conversation and godliness, Looking for and hasting unto the coming of the day of God, wherein the heavens being on fire shall be dissolved, and the elements shall melt with fervent heat? Nevertheless we, according to his promise, look for new heavens and a new earth, wherein dwelleth righteousness. Wherefore, beloved, seeing that ye look for such things, be diligent that ye may be found of him in peace, without spot, and blameless.

(2 Peter 3:10-14 KJV)

NOTHING CAN STOP THIS SEED

Being born again, not of corruptible seed, but of incorruptible, by the word of God, which liveth and abideth forever.

(1 Peter 1:23 KJV)

THIS IS A CALL TO THE KINGDOM EVANGELIST. THIS CALL IS AWAY FROM ALL THAT DISTRACTS AND UNTO HIM FOR A LIFETIME LOVE AFFAIR.

And Jesus said unto them, Come ye after me, and I will make you to become fishers of men. And straightway they forsook their nets, and followed him.

(Mark 1:17-18 KJV)

THE KINGDOM IS MARKED BY "POWER"

The Greek word for "power" is "DUNAMIS" and refers to the might, ability, and strength of the Lord.

For the Kingdom of God is not in word, but in power.

(1 Cor. 4:20 KJV)

THE POWER TO:

- Change the way we live
- Confront
- Convict
- Convert
- Deliver
- Restore to wholeness (ministry of reconciliation)

CHAPTER SEVEN

Kingdom Evangelism is With Dominion

Evangelism is the life of God working in and through His people, the Church of the Lord Jesus Christ, the Lord in the earth. THAT'S YOU!!!!

For the eyes of the Lord are over the righteous, and his ears are open unto their prayers: but the face of the Lord is against them that do evil. And who is he that will harm you, if ye be followers of that which is good? But and if ye suffer for righteousness' sake, happy are ye: and be not afraid of their terror, neither be troubled; But sanctify the Lord God in your hearts: and be ready always to give an answer to every man that asketh you a reason of the hope that is in you with meekness and fear: Having a good conscience; that, whereas they speak evil of you, as of evildoers, they may be ashamed that falsely accuse your good conversation in Christ. For it is better, if the will of God be so, that ye suffer for well doing, than for evil doing.

(1 Pet. 3:12-17 KJV)

Today we must express the same kind of Love that Jesus expressed in His life. Love is what's missing in the church. The key to "why" and "how" we Evangelize, is the Love of God.

UNTIL YOU CAN LOVE THEM YOU CAN NEVER WIN THEM.

WHY SHOULD WE EVANGELIZE? It's the Commandment of God.

And Jesus came and spake unto them, saying, All power is given unto me in heaven and in earth. Go ye therefore, and teach all nations, baptizing them in the name of the Father, and of the Son, and of the Holy Ghost. Teaching them to observe all things whatsoever I have commanded you: and, lo, I am with you always, even unto the end of the world. Amen.

(Matt. 28:18-20 KJV)

HOW SHOULD WE EVANGELIZE?

1. The most obvious answer would be to preach the word of God or tell them what the Bible says. That may be true, but exactly how should it be done?

- Tell people with honesty that they need to change their minds about God.

- They must believe the gospel, there is no other way.

- Salvation is a free gift to anyone that believes.

- It doesn't cost you anything; the price has already been paid in full, if you can believe it. (Romans 3:23, 6:23, 10:9-10)

- We must be accurate in what we say, because only the truth will make anyone free.

(John 8:32)

2. We must tell people the truth with a degree of urgency, expressing to them that the time is NOW! Today is the day of salvation.

For he is our God; and we are the people of his pasture, and the sheep of his hand. Today if ye will hear his voice, harden not your heart, as in the provocation, and as in the day of temptation in the wilderness:
(Ps. 95:7-8 KJV)

Again, he limiteth a certain day, saying in David, Today, after so long a time; as it is said, Today if ye will hear his voice, harden not your hearts. For if Jesus had given them rest, then would he not afterward have spoken of another day. There remaineth therefore a rest to the people of God.
(Heb. 4:7-9 KJV)

JESUS IS THE ONLY WAY BACK TO GOD FOR ANYONE!

Jesus saith unto him, I am the way, the truth, and the life: no man cometh unto the Father, but by me.
(John 14:6 KJV)

Neither is there salvation in any other: for there is none other name under heaven given among men, whereby we must be saved.
(Acts 4:12 KJV)

That if thou shalt confess with thy mouth the Lord Jesus, and shalt believe in thine heart that God hath raised him from the dead, thou shalt be saved.
(Rom. 10:9 KJV)

AFTER SALVATION, WE MUST LEARN TO TRUST IN GOD

Trust in the LORD with all thine heart; and lean not unto thine own understanding.In all thy ways acknowledge him, and he shall direct thy paths.

(Prov. 3:5-6KJV)

3. We must testify to people with joy how God changed us and we haven't been the same since. Your testimony should provoke in them a willingness to not want to allow another day to pass without experiencing this joy.

They must know that by coming to Christ they will:

- Gain a relationship with God the Father, the Creator of all things.

- Gain the forgiveness for every sin or short-coming they ever had.

- Gain a meaningful life and a reason for living.

- Receive purpose and begin to discover why they were born.

- Discover that they are the purpose and the program of God. (God is building us for "His" dwelling place in the Earth).

- Receive the freedom to serve God without fear or religious strongholds. (John 6:36)

- Be received into the Family of God by birth. (Eph. 3:15)

- Receive certainty and assurance. Hope maketh not ashamed. (Rom. 5:5)

4. You should use the Bible to:

- Learn for yourself and share it with others

- Show that you are not speaking "your mind" but the mind of God.

- Purchase a small Bible to witness with (this will take away the fear of intimidation)

- Remember to pray for the people before you meet them

THE MOST IMPORTANT PART OF EVANGELISM IS INTERCESSORY PRAYER.

BECAUSE SALVATION IS THE WORK OF GOD, WE MUST HAVE A LOVE FOR THE LOST!

But when he saw the multitudes, he was moved with compassion on them, because they fainted, and were scattered abroad, as sheep having no shepherd. Then saith he unto his disciples, The harvest truly is plenteous, but the labourers are few; Pray ye therefore the Lord of the harvest, that he will send forth labourers into his harvest.
(Matt. 9:36-38KJV)

Brethren, my heart's desire and prayer to God for Israel is that they might be saved.
(Rom. 10:1 KJV)

For Christ is the end of the law for righteousness to every one that believeth.
(Rom. 10:4 KJV)

GOD IS NOT WILLING THAT ANY SHOULD PERISH!

THE KINGDOM OF GOD AND KINGDOM EVANGELISM IS:

- The Dominion of God
- The Rule of God
- A Government

EVERY KINGDOM HAS A PEOPLE OR AN ETHNIC GROUP THAT IDENTIFIES WITH ITS OPERATION. IN ORDER FOR ITS OPERATION TO BE SUCCESSFUL, THERE MUST BE:

PREPARATION: To make or get ready, to put together or to compound; "Man and God in One."

SPONTANEITY: Spontaneously done, produced, or occurring; naturally or without planning.

RESPONSIBILITY: Responsible for acts or decisions, able to fulfill obligations, having important duties.

THE KINGDOM OF HEAVEN: The place or location of spiritual domain.

THE KINGDOM OF GOD: The person to whom the Kingdom belongs.

THIS KINGDOM AUTHORITY COMES FROM GOD TO THE PLACE WHERE HE IS TO RULE; WITHIN YOU FOR YOU TO WALK IN POWER.

THIS KINGDOM AUTHORITY:

* Brings man into submission and gives him God's ability.

* Brings about the fulfillment of God's will.

* Is the UNION of God and Man as one being.

* Is within you.

THIS IS THE SOVEREIGNTY OF GOD THAT IS OVER ALL THINGS; "THERE IS NO ESCAPE."

Neither shall they say, Lo here! or, lo there! for, behold, the Kindom of God is within you.
(Luke 17:21 KJV)

Ask, and it shall be given you; seek, and ye shall find; knock, and it shall be opened unto you: For every one that asketh receiveth; and he that seeketh findeth; and to him that knocketh it shall be opened.
(Matt. 7:7-9 KJV)

Enter ye in at the strait gate: for wide is the gate, and broad is the way, that leadeth to destruction, and many there be which go in thereat: Because strait is the gate, and narrow is the way, which leadeth unto life, and few there be that find it.
(Matt. 7:13-14 KJV)

Not every one that saith unto me, Lord, Lord, shall enter into the Kingdom of heaven; but he that doeth the will of my Father which is in heaven. Many will say to me in that day,

Lord, Lord, have we not prophesied in thy name? and in thy name have cast out devils? and in thy name done many wonderful works? And then will I profess unto them, I never knew you: depart from me, ye that work iniquity. Therefore whosoever heareth these sayings of mine, and doeth them, I will liken him unto a wise man, which built his house upon a rock: And the rain descended, and the floods came, and the winds blew, and beat upon that house; and it fell not: for it was founded upon a rock.

(Matt. 7:21-25 KJV)

CHAPTER EIGHT

Rules in Righteousness

And I say also unto thee, That thou art Peter, and upon this rock I will build my church; and the gates of hell shall not prevail against it. And I will give unto thee the keys of the Kingdom of heaven: and whatsoever thou shalt bind on earth shall be bound in heaven: and whatsoever thou shalt loose on earth shall be loosed in heaven.

(Matthew 16:18-19 KJV)

CROSSOVER FROM PENTECOST TO THE GATHERING TOGETHER OF THE LOST SHEEP OF THE HOUSE OF ISRAEL.

BUILDING A RELATIONSHIP WITH A FATHER MINISTRY.

NETWORK PEOPLE OF THE SAME MIND, PURPOSE, AND DESIRE.

There must be an <u>Apostolic Reformation</u>. It must be declared from Apostolic Authority, because this is the time of the <u>Apostles</u>.

Go through, go through the gates; prepare ye the way of the people; cast up, cast up the highway; gather out the stones; lift up a standard for the people.

(Isa. 62:10 KJV)

The Kingdom of God must be executed through the very authority of the Government of God. The Government of God is the life and the spirit working through His <u>chosen earthen vessels</u>.

There must first be a relationship with God the Father; not the blood of the lamb, nor the love of the Son, but a relationship with the Father; through the blood of the lamb, by the love of the Son.

> *For God, the Father, so loved the world that He gave His Son.*
>
> (John 3:16 KJV)

KINGDOM IS GOD'S RULE IN RIGHTEOUSNESS

The Father sent the Kingdom of God from heaven and purposed to make the instrument for establishing a "Kingdom of Glory" among men.

> *And saying, Repent ye: for the Kingdom of heaven is at hand.*
>
> (Matt. 3:2 KJV)

> *The Kingdom consists not in these outward and indifferent things, neither does it particularly enjoin, nor forbid such. "For the Kingdom of God is not meat and drink; but righteousness, and peace, and joy in the Holy Ghost."*
>
> (Rom. 14:17 KJV)

But *RIGHTEOUSNESS*: Pardon of sin and holiness of heart and life.

And *PEACE*: In the soul from a sense of God's mercy; peace regulating, ruling, and harmonizing the heart without inward disturbance.

44

And *JOY IN THE HOLY SPIRIT*: Solid spiritual happiness; a joy, which springs from a clear sense of God's mercy; the love of God being shed abroad in the heart by the Holy Spirit without any kind of mental agony or defeat.

In other words, it is happiness brought into the soul by the Holy Spirit, and maintained there by the same. This is heaven in earth; righteousness without sin or distressing fear.

> *For he that in these things serveth Christ is acceptable to God, and approved of men. Let us therefore follow after the things which make for peace, and things wherewith one may edify another.*
>
> (Rom. 14:18-19 KJV)

> *And ye shall be unto me a Kingdom of priests, and a holy nation. These are the Words which thou shalt speak unto the children of Israel.*
>
> (Ex. 19:6 KJV)

> *For the Kingdom is the LORD's: and he is the governor among the nations.*
>
> (Ps. 22:28 KJV)

> *The LORD hath prepared his throne in the heavens; and his Kingdom ruleth over all.*
>
> (Ps. 103:19 KJV)

> *Thy Kingdom is everlasting, and thy dominion endureth throughout all Generations.*
>
> (Ps. 145:13 KJV)

> *And lead us not into temptation, but deliver us from evil: For thine is the Kingdom , and*

the power, and the glory, forever. Amen.
(Matt. 6:13 KJV)

But seek ye first the Kingdom of God, and his righteousness; and all these things shall be added unto you.
(Matt. 6:33 KJV)

And this gospel of the Kingdom shall be preached in all the world for a witness unto all nations; and then shall the end come.
(Matt. 24:14 KJV)

The law and the prophets were until John: since that time the Kingdom of God is preached, and every man presseth into it.
(Luke 16:16 KJV)

Jesus answered, My Kingdom is not of this world: if my kingdom were of this world, then would my servants fight, that I should not be delivered to the Jews: but now is my kingdom not from hence.
(John 18:36 KJV)

Nor thieves, nor covetous, nor drunkards, nor revilers, nor extortioners, shall inherit the Kingdom of God.
(1 Cor. 6:10 KJV)

REPENT FOR THE KINGDOM OF GOD IS HERE

In those days came John the Baptist, preaching in the wilderness of Judaea, And saying, Repent ye: for the Kingdom of heaven is at hand.
(Matt. 3:1-2 KJV)

I indeed baptize you with water unto repentance: but he that cometh after me is mightier than I, whose shoes I am not worthy to remove; he shall baptize you with the Holy Ghost, and with fire.

(Matt. 3:11 KJV)

NOW IS THE TIME TO WALK AND LIVE IN THE REALITY AND AUTHORITY OF THE KINGDOM ABSENT FROM THE TEMPTATIONS OF THE WORLD.

There are three areas to be tempted or tested and all of them are of the flesh.

1. The Lust of the Flesh.
2. The Lust of the Eyes.
3. The Pride of Life.

Then saith Jesus unto him, Get thee hence, Satan: for it is written, Thou shalt worship the Lord thy God, and him only shalt thou serve. Then the devil leaveth him, and, behold, angels came and ministered unto him.

(Matt. 4:10-11 KJV)

THE END RESULT WAS THAT THE DEVIL COULD FIND NOTHING IN HIM.

And when the devil had ended all the temptation, he departed from him for a season. And Jesus returned in the power of the Spirit into Galilee, and there went out a fame of him through all the region round about. And he taught in their synagogues, being glorified of all. And he came to

Nazareth, where he had been brought up, and as his custom was, he went into the synagogue on the sabbath day, and stood up to read.

And there was delivered unto him the book of the prophet Esaias. And when he had opened the book, he found the place where it was written, the Spirit of the Lord is upon me, because he hath anointed me to preach the gospel to the poor; he hath sent me to heal the brokenhearted, to preach deliverance to the captives, recovering of sight to the blind, to set at liberty them that are bruised, and to preach the acceptable year of the Lord.

And he closed the book, and he gave it again to the minister, and sat down. And the eyes of all them that were in the synagogue were fastened on him. And he began to say unto them, This day is this scripture fulfilled in your ears. And all bare him witness, and wondered at the gracious words which proceeded out of his mouth. And they said, Is not this Joseph's son? And he said unto them, Ye will surely say unto me this proverb, Physician, heal thyself: whatsoever we have heard done in Capernaum, do also here in thy country. And he said, Verily I say unto you, No prophet is accepted in his own country.

(Luke 4:13-24 KJV)

EVERY BELOVED MUST LOSE HIS HEAD

John the beloved was cast into prison because he had to lose his head (his way of thinking) in order for Jesus to come forth.

Now when Jesus had heard that John was cast into prison, he departed into Galilee; And leaving Nazareth, he came and dwelt in Capernaum, which is upon the sea coast, in the borders of Zabulon and Nephthalim: That it might be fulfilled which was spoken by Esaias the prophet, saying, The land of Zabulon, and the land of Nephthalim, by the way of the sea, beyond Jordan, Galilee of the Gentiles; The people which sat in darkness saw great light; and to them which sat in the region and shadow of death light is sprung up.

(Matt. 4:12-16 KJV)

ZEBULON (habitation): This speaks of the experience of your Christianity leaving the individual realm causing your thinking to change from I, to We, to Him.

NEPHTHALIM (wrestling/struggle): This speaks of the experience of being an overcomer who is releasing the creative word with life as their credential.

AFTER REPENTENCE, THE FOCUS CHANGES FROM JOHN TO JESUS.

From that time Jesus began to preach, and to say, Repent: for the Kingdom of heaven is at hand. And Jesus, walking by the sea of Galilee, saw two brethren, Simon called Peter, and Andrew his brother, casting a net into the sea: for they were fishers. And he saith unto them, Follow me, and I will make you fishers of men.

(Matt. 4:17-19 KJV)

Wherefore henceforth know we no man after the flesh: yea, though we have known Christ after the flesh, yet now henceforth know we him no more. <u>Therefore if any man be in Christ, he is a new creature: old things are passed away; behold, all things are become new</u>.

(2 Cor. 5:16-17 KJV)

THEIR RESPONSE: They immediately left their nets and followed Him.

And they straightway left their nets, and followed him. And going on from thence, he saw other two brethren, James the son of Zebedee, and John his brother, in a ship with Zebedee their father, mending their nets; and he called them. And they immediately left the ship and their father, and followed him.

(Matt. 4:20-22 KJV)

And Jesus went about all Galilee, teaching in their synagogues, and preaching the gospel of the kingdom, and healing all manner of sickness and all manner of disease among the people. And his fame went throughout all Syria: and they brought unto him all sick people that were taken with divers diseases and torments, and those which were possessed with devils, and those which were lunatick, and those that had the palsy; and he healed them.

(Matt. 4:23-24)

And seeing the multitudes, he went up into a mountain: and when he was set, his disciples came unto him. And he opened his mouth, and taught them, saying:

Blessed are the poor in spirit, for theirs is the Kingdom of heaven.

Blessed are they that mourn, for they shall be comforted.

Blessed are the meek, for they shall inherit the earth.

Blessed are they which do hunger and thirst after righteousness, for they shall be filled.

Blessed are the merciful, for they shall obtain mercy.

Blessed are the pure in heart, for they shall see God.

Blessed are the peacemakers, for they shall be called the children of God.

Blessed are they which are persecuted for righteousness' sake, for theirs is the Kingdom of heaven.

Blessed are ye, when men shall revile you, and persecute you, and shall say all manner of evil against you falsely, for my sake.

Ye are the salt of the earth: but if the salt have lost his savour, wherewith shall it be salted? it is thenceforth good for nothing, but to be cast out, and to be trodden under foot of men.
                                        (Matt. 5:1-13 KJV)

REJOICE, AND BE EXCEEDING GLAD: FOR GREAT IS YOUR REWARD IN HEAVEN: FOR SO PERSECUTED THEY THE PROPHETS WHICH WERE BEFORE YOU.

You may contact Dr. McAllister at:

Dr. Bobby G. McAllister
PO Box 7179
Jacksonville, NC 28546

(910) 324-3360

bmcallister@ec.rr.com